Copyright © 2014 Hallmark Licensing, LLC

Published by Hallmark Gift Books,
a division of Hallmark Cards, Inc.,
Kansas City, MO 64141
Visit us on the Web at Hallmark.com.

All rights reserved. No part of this publication may be reproduced, transmitted, or stored in any form or by any means without the prior written permission of the publisher.

Editorial Director: Carrie Bolin
Editor: Kim Schworm Acosta
Art Director: Chris Opheim
Designers: Chris Grine & Jack Pullen
Production Design: Dan Horton
Written by: Chris Brethwaite
Contributing Writers: Linda Barnes, Suzanne Berry, Andrew Blackburn, Ellen Brenneman, Meg Burik, Bev Carlson, Renee Daniels, Stacey Donovan, Andre du Broc, Jennifer Fujita, Bill Gray, Suzanne Heins, Diana Manning, Tom Shay-Zapien, Dan Taylor, Drew Wagner, Molly Wigand, John Wurth

ISBN: 978-1-59530-741-5
BOK2169

Printed and bound in China
AUG14

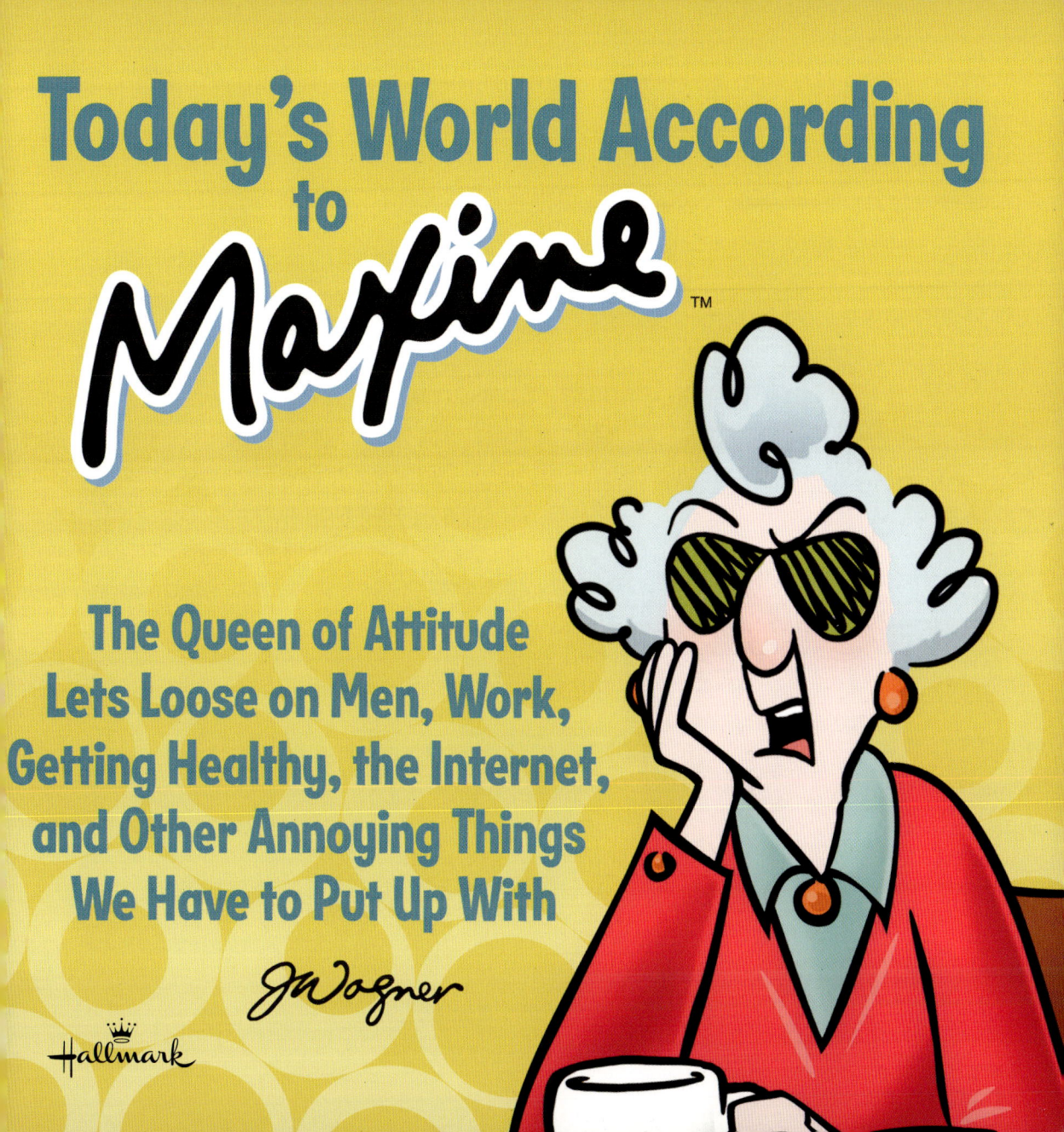

Table of Contents

Men: Gotta Love 'Em (Can't Do Much Else With 'Em)
p. 6

I'll Drink (and Eat) to That!
p. 22

No Pain, No Problem
p. 40

So Much Work, So Little Time to Complain
p. 56

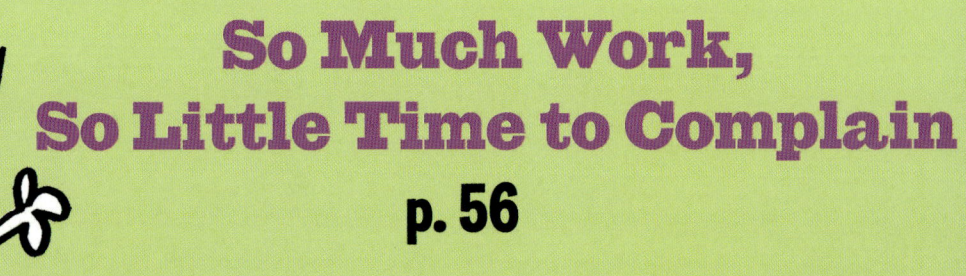

Older, but Whinier
p. 74

People Say the Dumbest Things
p. 90

Dollars and No Sense
p. 108

And Now a Word About Technology ... #@%&!
p. 124

Men: Gotta Love 'Em

(Can't Do Much Else With 'Em)

They say it's a man's world. And taking a quick look around the old planet, that would certainly explain a lot. Yes, what can you say about men that doesn't immediately conjure up a string of four-letter words— probably not a whole lot. But a good belly laugh? Just read the following and judge for yourself.

(and Eat) to That!

I'm something of a foodie in that I'm picky about what I eat. If it isn't high in fat and calories you're not going to find it on my plate. Hey, if the man upstairs wanted me to eat healthy, he'd have given me a cottontail and floppy ears. And don't get me started on drinking. On second thought, please get me started on drinking.

I'm throwing a
wine and cheese
party tonight.
Only for myself.
And without
the cheese.
JWagner

I'm slowly learning Spanish. I started with "burrito" and now I'm up to "tequila." Olé!

The main point of a cruise is to eat until you weigh the same as the boat.
JWagner

No Pain,

No Problem

I've been in shape for quite a few years. Unfortunately, it's the shape of an old lady. My feeling is that if I have enough strength to wrestle the cardboard lid off a half-gallon tub of triple fudge ripple, I've got nothing to worry about. Well, except maybe clogged arteries and passing out after climbing up a stair or two, says my doctor. But why should I believe *him?* I'm still trying to figure out who can cure my enlarged medical bill.

If I ever get a
heart transplant,
I'd want my ex's.
It's never
been used.
JWagner

Wouldn't it be nice if retail therapy was covered by health insurance?
JWagner

I'd like to work some cardio into my daily routine. But all the eatio and sleepio doesn't leave much time.
gWagner

I just found out
I have IBES...
Irritable Because of
Everything
Syndrome.
JWagner

My favorite day of the week to exercise will always be tomorrow.

I was planning to go to the gym, but I got a better offer from my refrigerator.

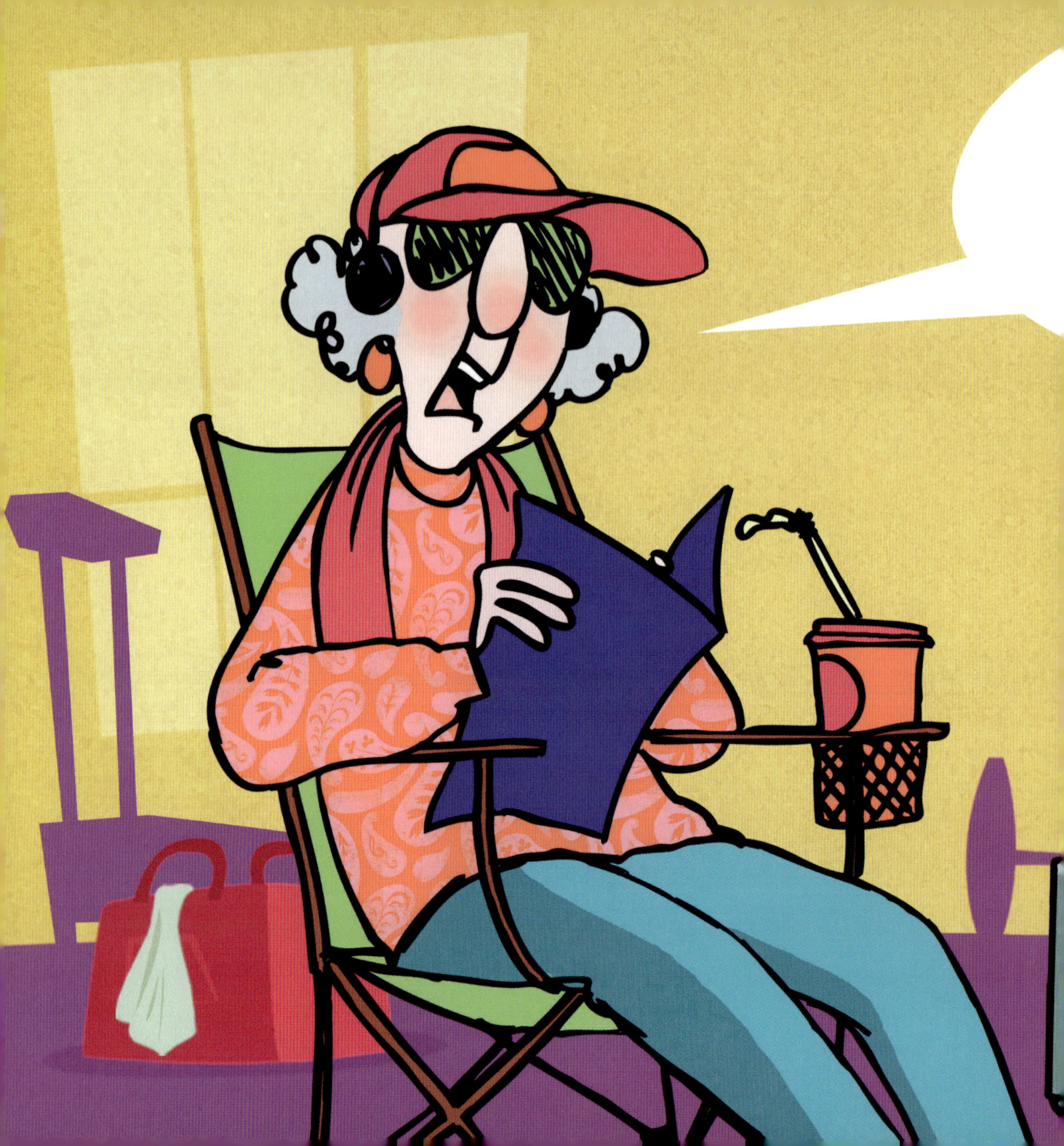

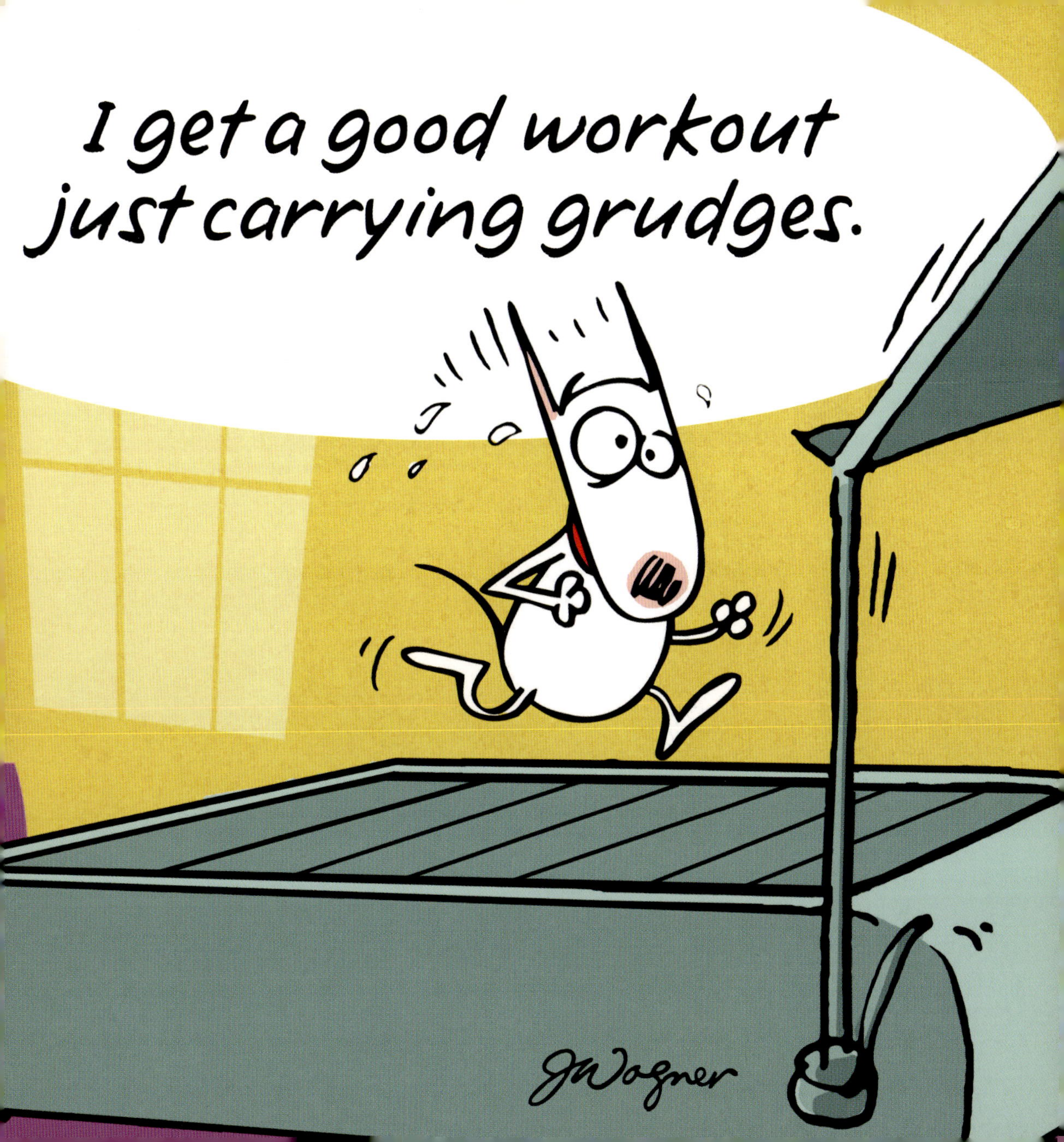
I get a good workout
just carrying grudges.
JWagner

My doctor asked me if I've ever had a stress test. Sure ... it's called LIFE!

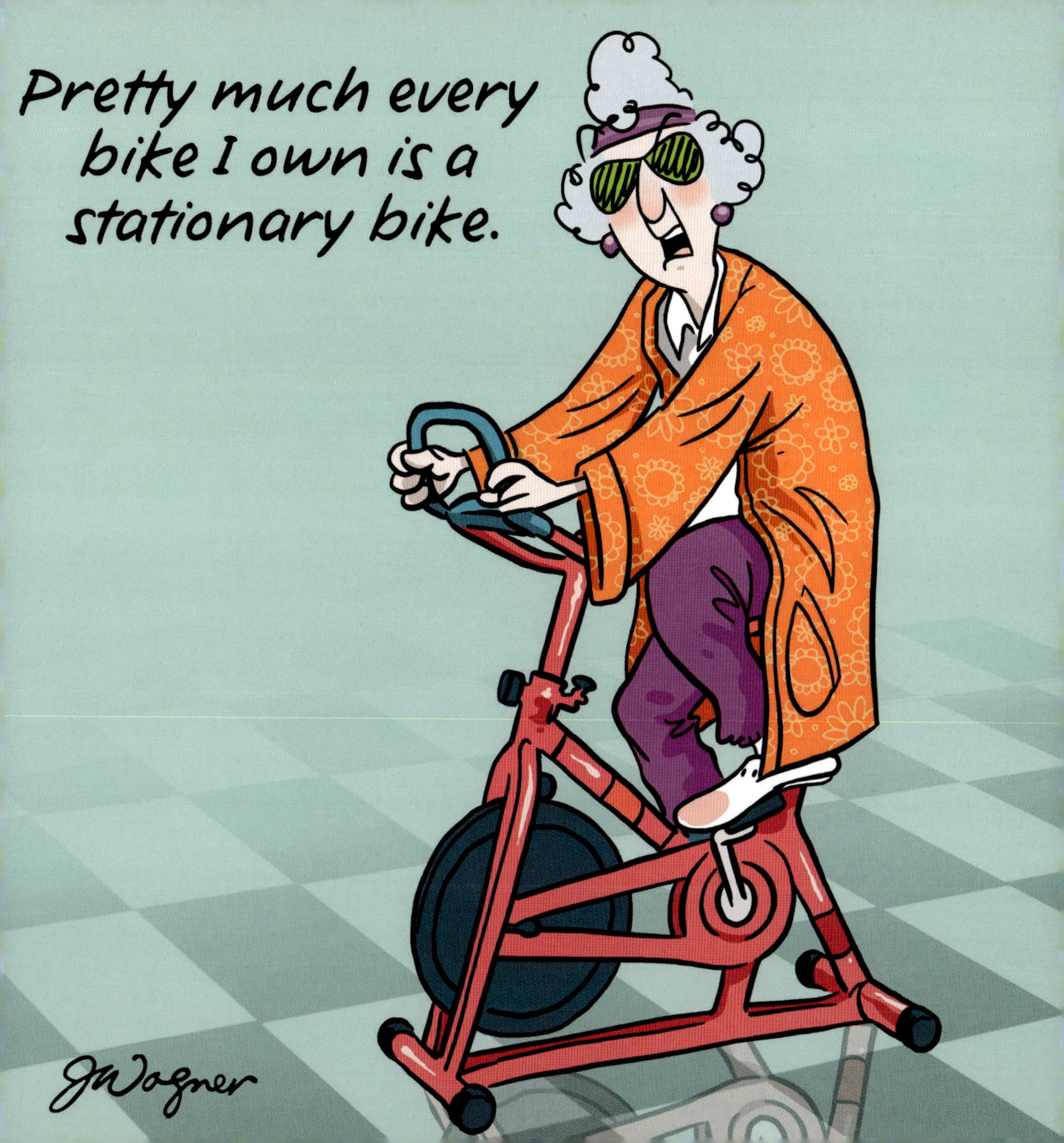
Pretty much every bike I own is a stationary bike.
JWagner

My doctor said to eat better. I told him with what he charges, I'm lucky I eat at all.
JWagner

They say you're supposed to listen to your body, but we stopped talking years ago."

In my day, lots of people did yoga. Back then it was called "Twister."
JWagner

My doctor's concerned about my high blood pressure. I told him next time don't leave me sitting in the waiting room for two hours.
DOCTOR

So Much Work, So Little

Time to Complain

I'll be honest, I don't mind going to work. It's the eight hours I spend there that kills me. Actually, work gives you a sense of purpose in life. It also gives you headaches, ulcers, and enough stress to pop diamonds out your you-know-what, but I digress. So grab a five-dollar latte, kick off your shoes, and pretend the boss just called in to say he'll be late.

I got a part-time job as a store greeter. But apparently, "You again?" isn't the greeting they had in mind.
GETMORE
welcome
JWagner

When I'm stressed out, nothing helps like a long, hot bath. Unfortunately, they frown on that at work.
SOAP
JWagner

Ever notice the same people who want you to think outside the box expect you to work in a cubicle?

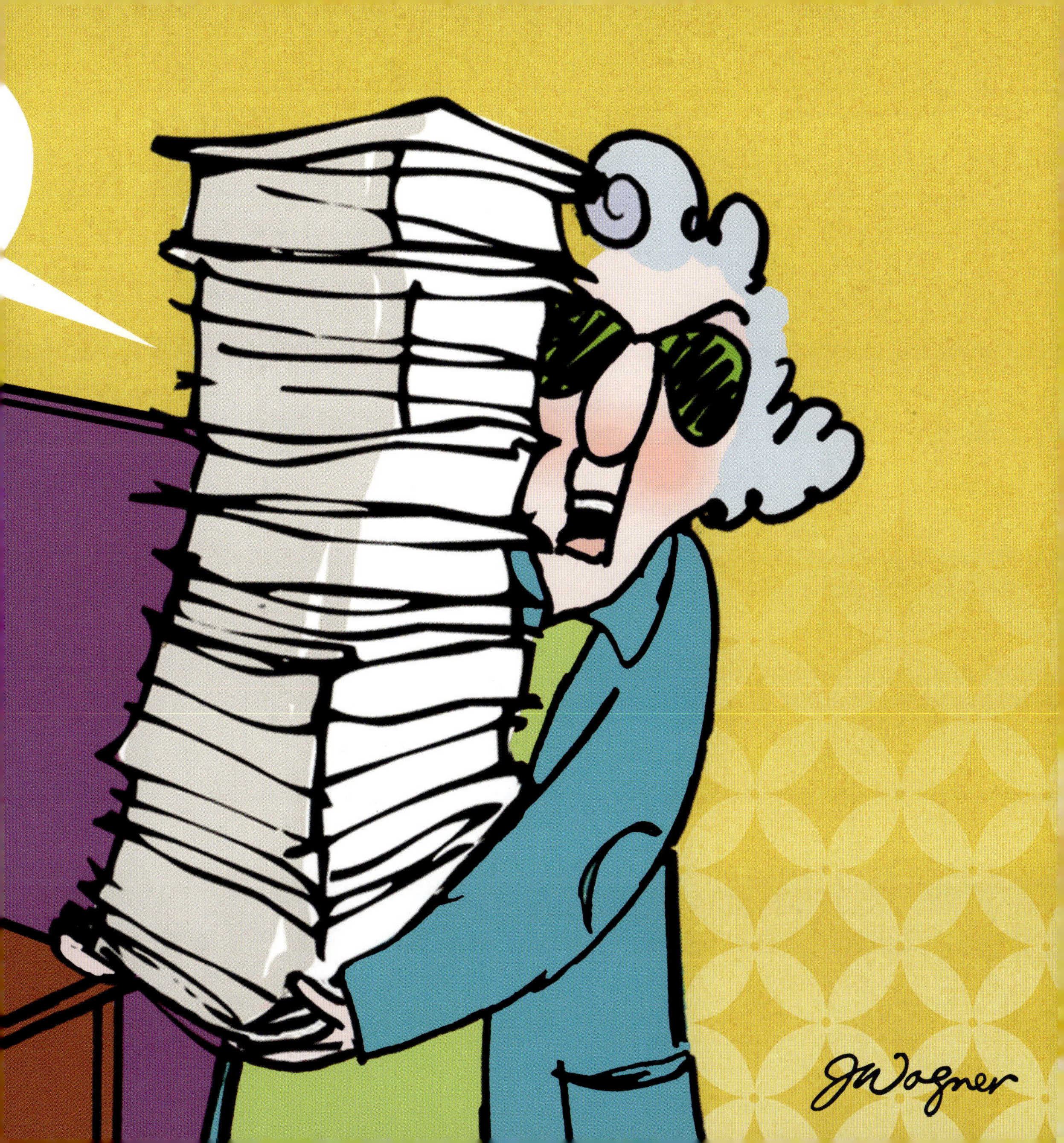
JWagner

I don't know why it's called a "break room." It's always full of people I need a break from.
I ♥ MY ATTITUDE PROBLEM
JWagner

My boss told me I should dress for the job I want. What does a stay-at-home billionaire wear?

Some mornings, if I came into work any later, I'd be on the night shift.
JWagner

A lot of my co-workers have already retired ... they just haven't told their boss yet.

"I need my eight hours of sleep. But my boss keeps wantin' me to do my job."

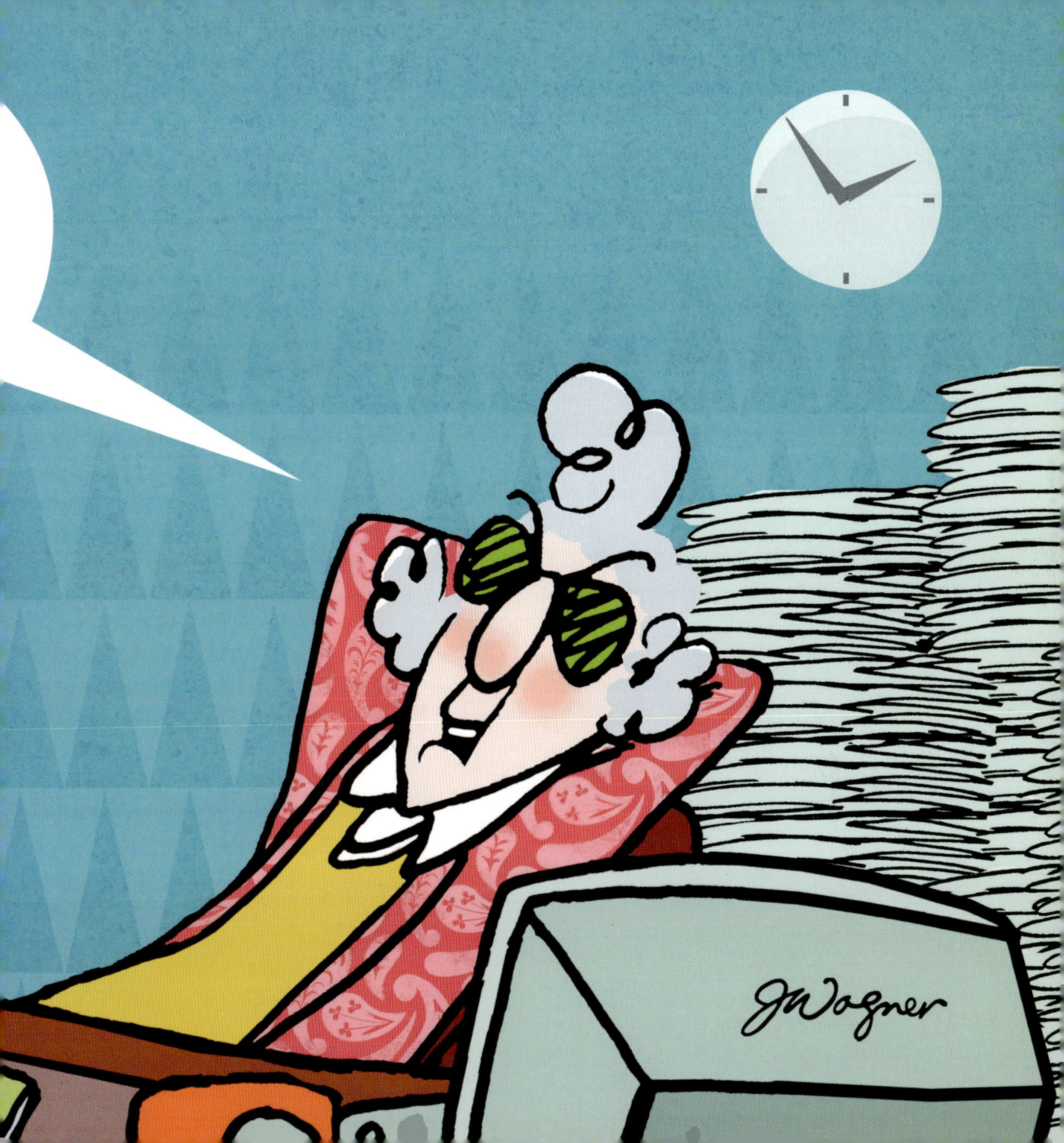
JWagner

There's no "I" in "TEAM," but there's always at least one big "A," if you know what I mean.
I ♥ MY ATTITUDE PROBLEM

My co-workers say they get a lot done working from home. Yeah, a lot of laundry, shopping, and daytime TV.
I ♥ MY ATTITUDE PROBLEM
JWagner

There's no excuse for laziness, but if you find one, let me know.
JWagner

If you can't say something nice about
omeone, you probably
work where I do.

When I argue with my boss, I always have the last word. Luckily, he never hears it.
IN

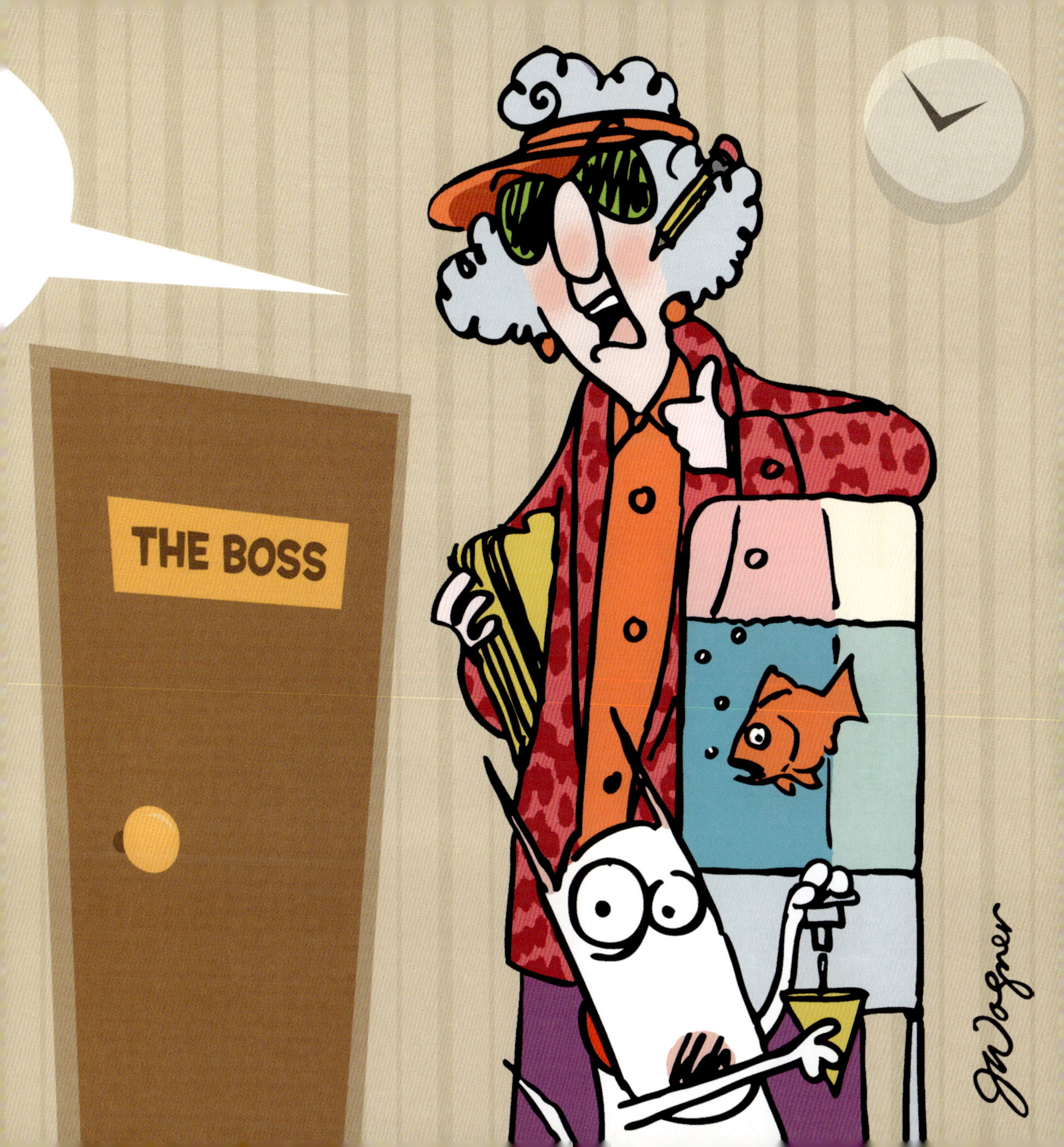
THE BOSS

Older,

but Whinier

Time marches on, and judging by how I feel, it's doubled back a time or two. And though there's nothing we can do about all the things that droop, sag, ache, and wrinkle, we can still shake our fist at Mother Nature— and hopefully without seeing too much flabby arm jiggle. Now, what was I saying?

"I'm getting to the age where visiting old friends requires a psychic medium!"

At my age, a "balanced lifestyle" means 50% aches and 50% pains.
JWagner

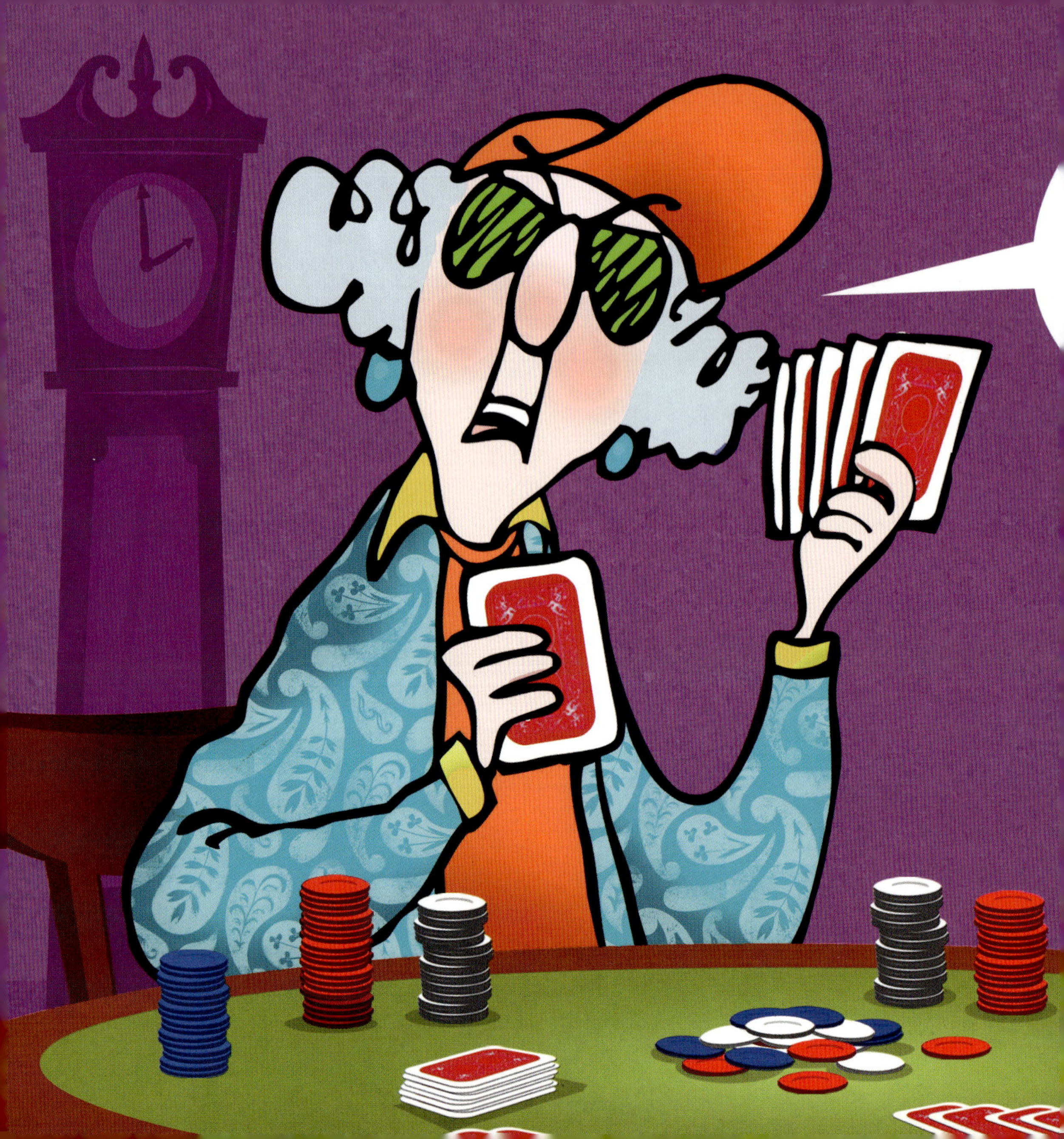

I still have a biological clock. It's on display in the Smithsonian.
gWagner

At my age, half the stuff in my shopping cart has a longer expiration date than I do.

I'm at the age now where every time I hear the song "Afternoon Delight," I think of a nap.
JWagner

Funny thing about getting older ... either you really hate it or you're really stupid.

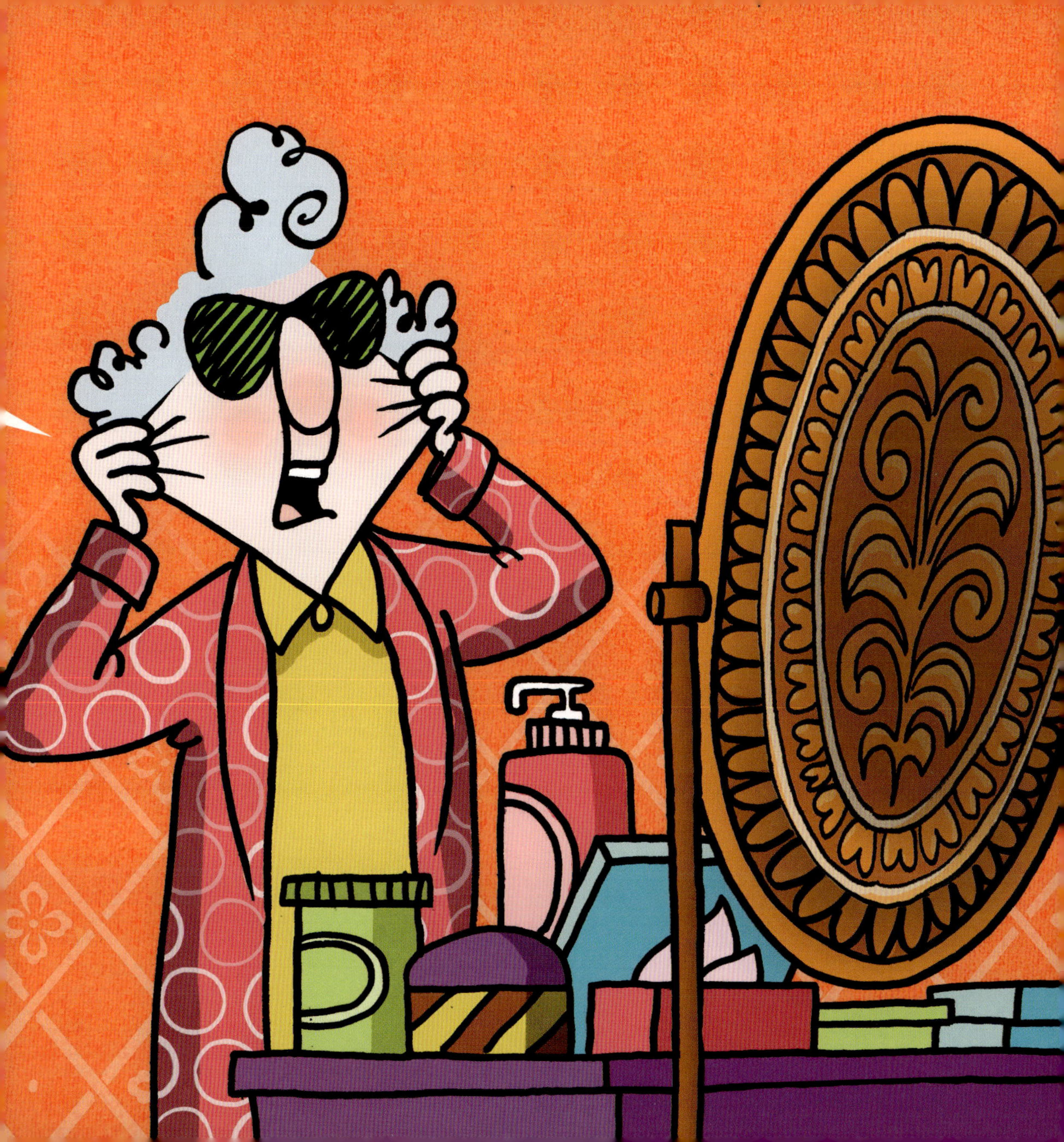

I still go out a lot at night...
out of bed to use
the bathroom.
JWagner

At my age, a "party favor" means somebody helping me out of a low-slung chair.
JWagner

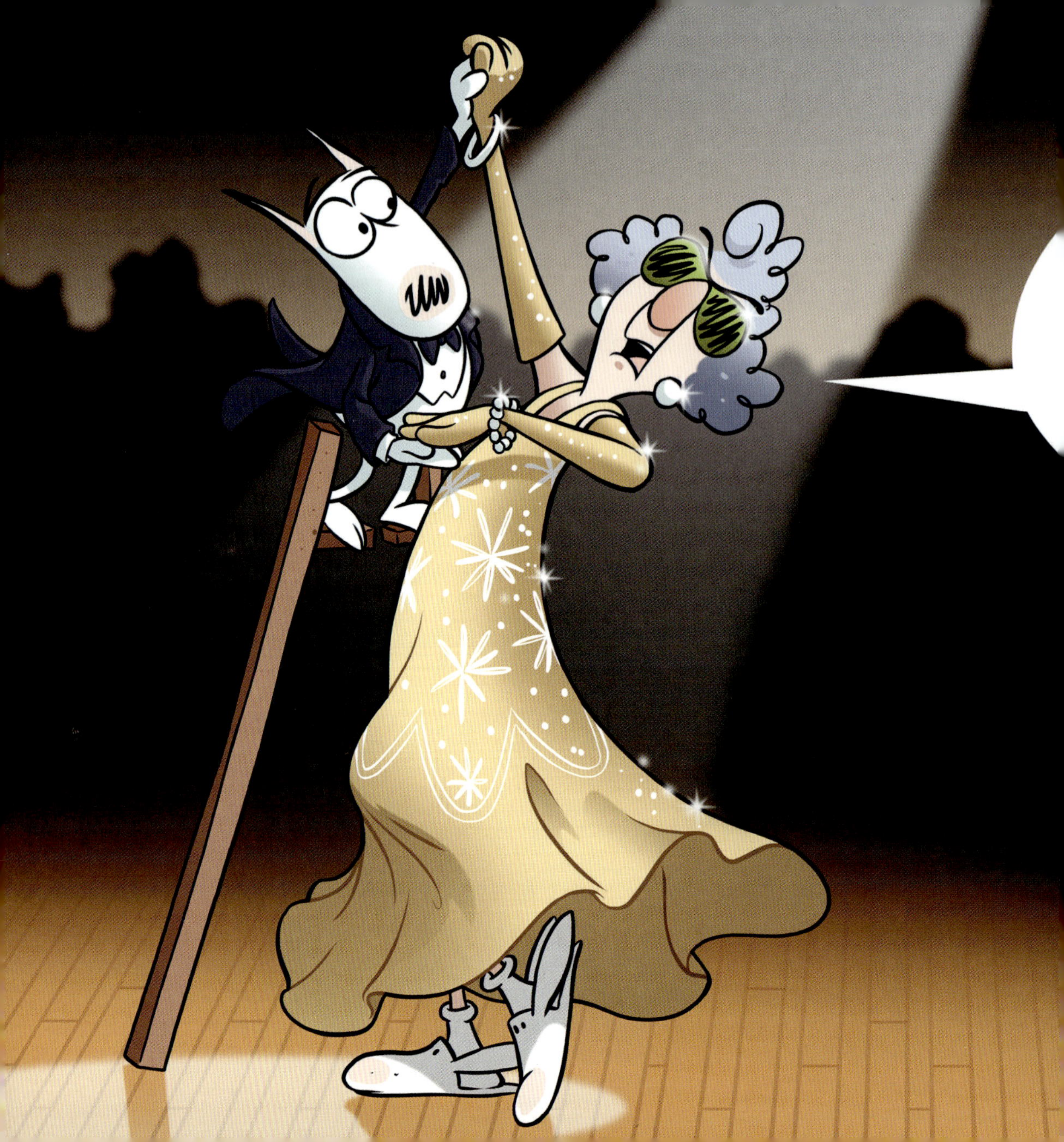

I can still burn up the ol' dance floor. Stupid hot flashes!

At my age, I've learned to look for love in all the right places ... the refrigerator, the microwave, the oven ...
JWagner

When I was young, I used to hope I'd wake up beautiful. Now I just hope I wake up!
JWagner

People Say

the Dumbest Things

I wish it weren't the case, but some people are difficult and hard to get along with. In fact, there's a name for these people: friends and relatives. And let's not forget everybody else we interact with on a daily basis who makes us want to commit road rage on the highway of life. In any event, we can't blame all of life's aggravations, frustrations, and disappointments on others, but we can certainly try.

Ever notice how the more closed-minded somebody is, the more open-mouthed they tend to be?
JWagner

When I'm out with friends, I think nothing of picking up the check ... and moving it closer to someone else.
JWagner

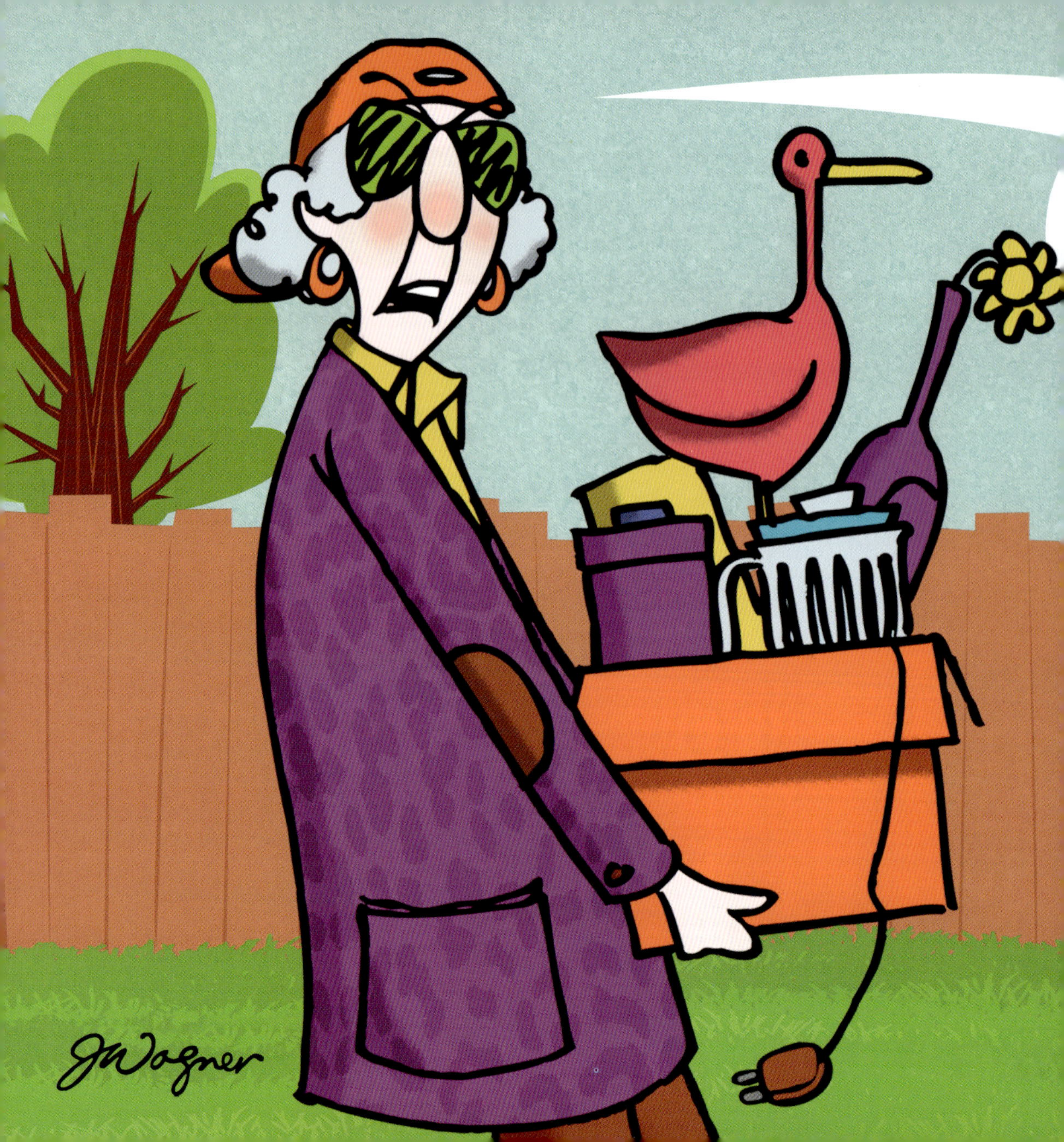
JWagner

Some friendships are so strong they can last right up until one of you needs help moving!

There's a special place in my heart for family. I think that explains the palpitations.
I ♥ MY ATTITUDE PROBLEM
JWagner

A cookout with the family can only mean one thing ... I'm gonna have to deal with lots of wieners!

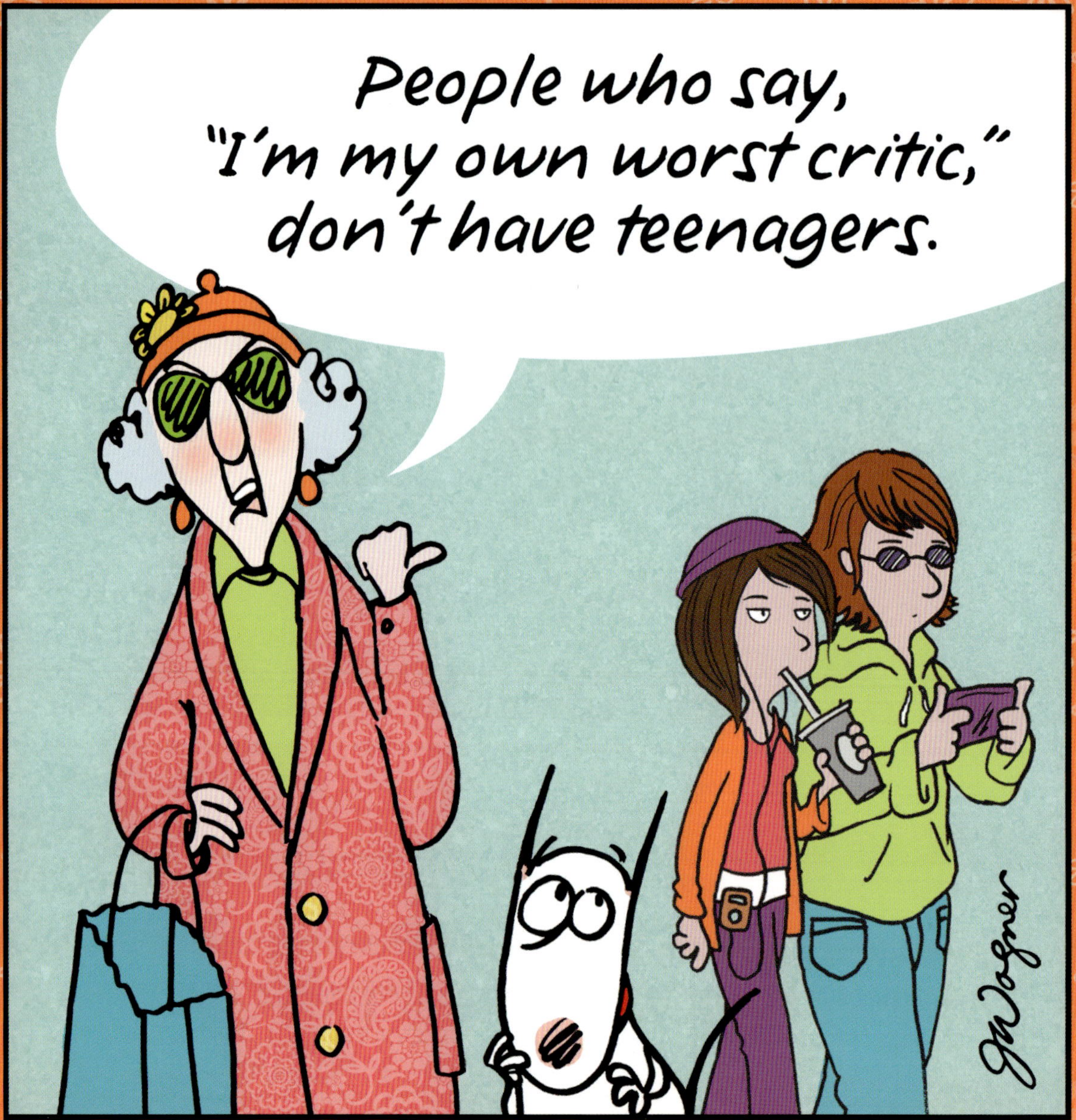
People who say, "I'm my own worst critic," don't have teenagers.

A good friend is like a margarita ...
a little sweet, a little salty,
and can knock you on your
butt when you need it.

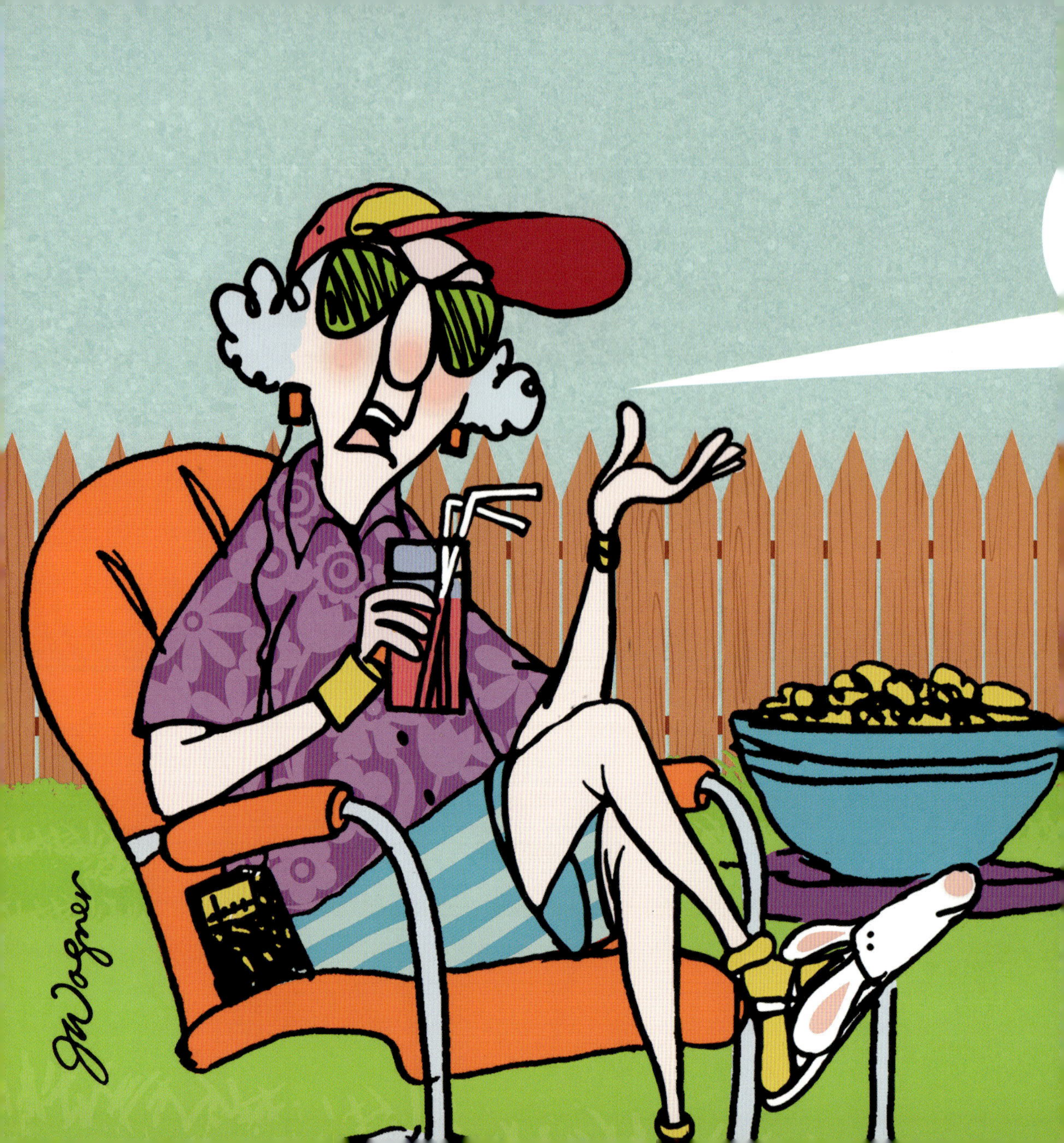

The day I mowed my first lawn was the day I understood why my mother wanted kids.

The best ship of all is friendship. The second best has gambling and free drinks.
JWagner

My idea of a "friend request" is telling my neighbor to get out of my yard.
I ♥ MY ATTITUDE PROBLEM
JWagner

I'm the peacemaker in my family. That should give you an idea of what the rest of my relatives are like.
JWagner

I'm going to try putting others first for a change. OK, that's long enough.
JWagner

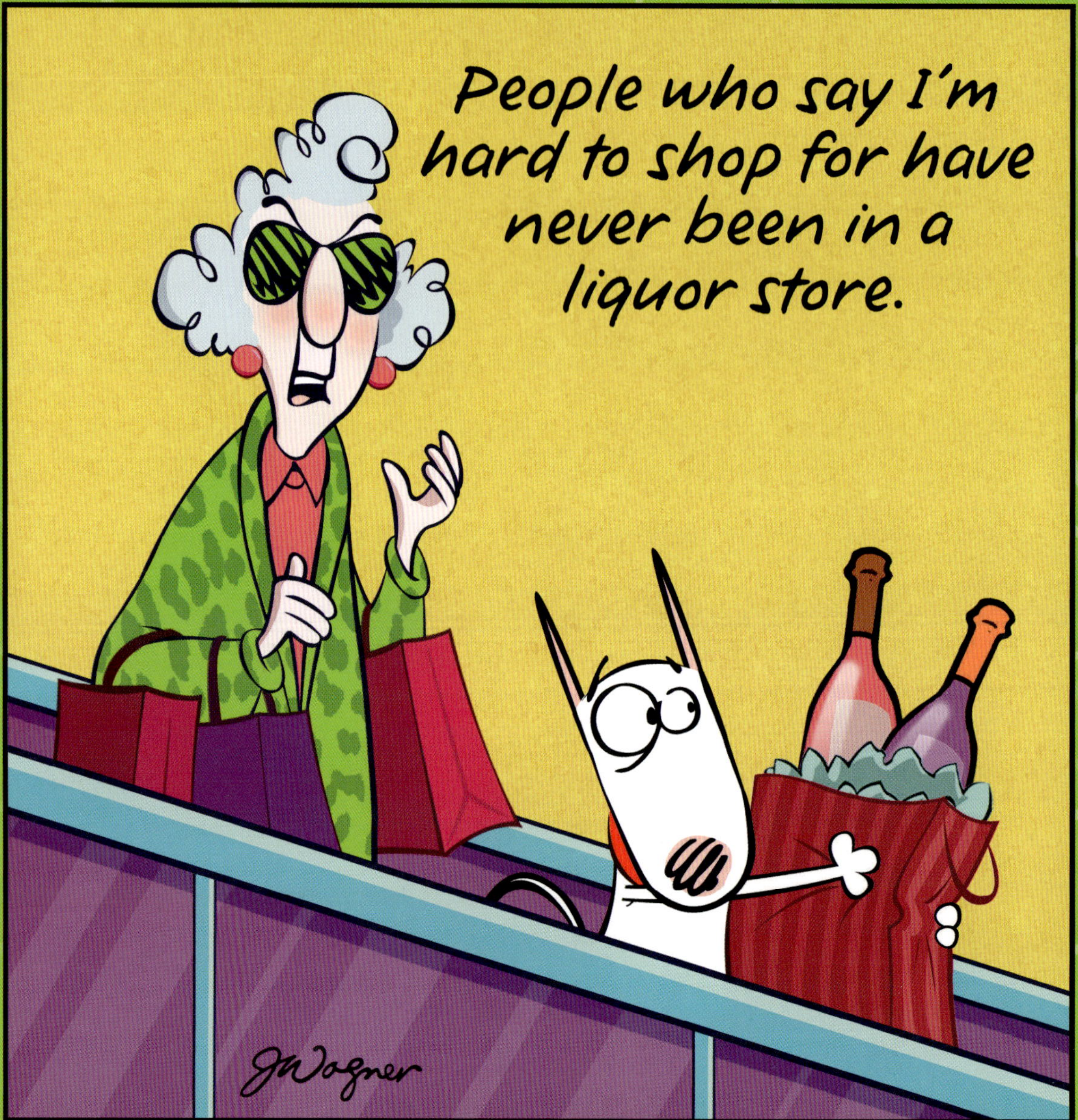
People who say I'm hard to shop for have never been in a liquor store.
JWagner

I don't understand why people pay shrinks. I'll tell them what's wrong with them for free.
JWagner

Dollars

and No Sense

Some people say it takes money to make money. I believe 'em—those color copiers don't come cheap. But seriously, financial security is one of the most important things in life. It's right up there with flushable wipes and boneless chicken wings. Fortunately, I'm one of the lucky ones. I have enough money to last the rest of my life. Or a week from Tuesday, whichever comes first.

Throwing money at your problems won't work ... unless I'm one of them.

My retirement fund is more of a "401 Not OK."
I ♥ MY ATTITUDE PROBLEM

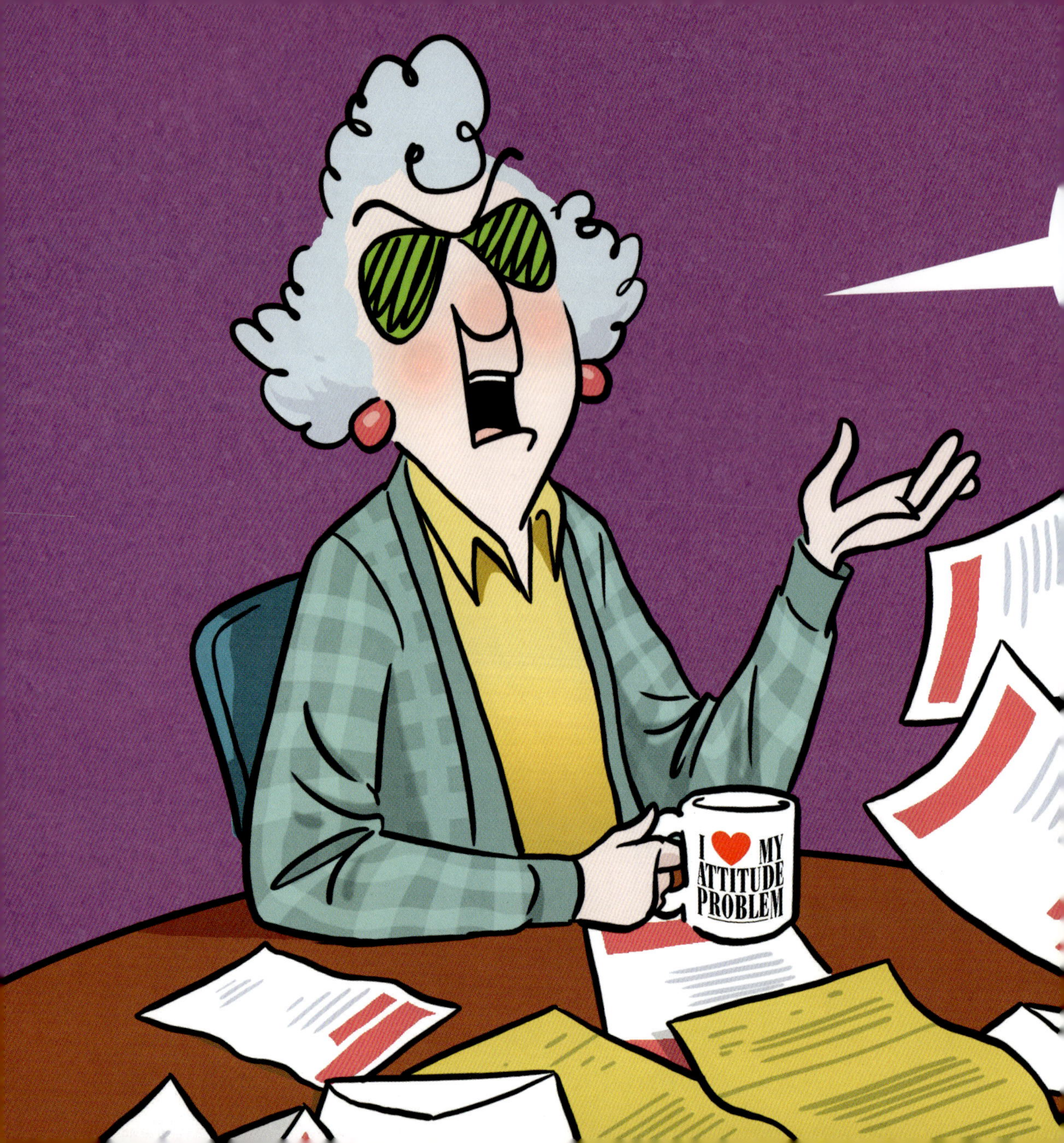
I ♥ MY
ATTITUDE
PROBLEM

I don't know why they call it a fixed income. After I pay everybody, I'm totally broke!
JWagner

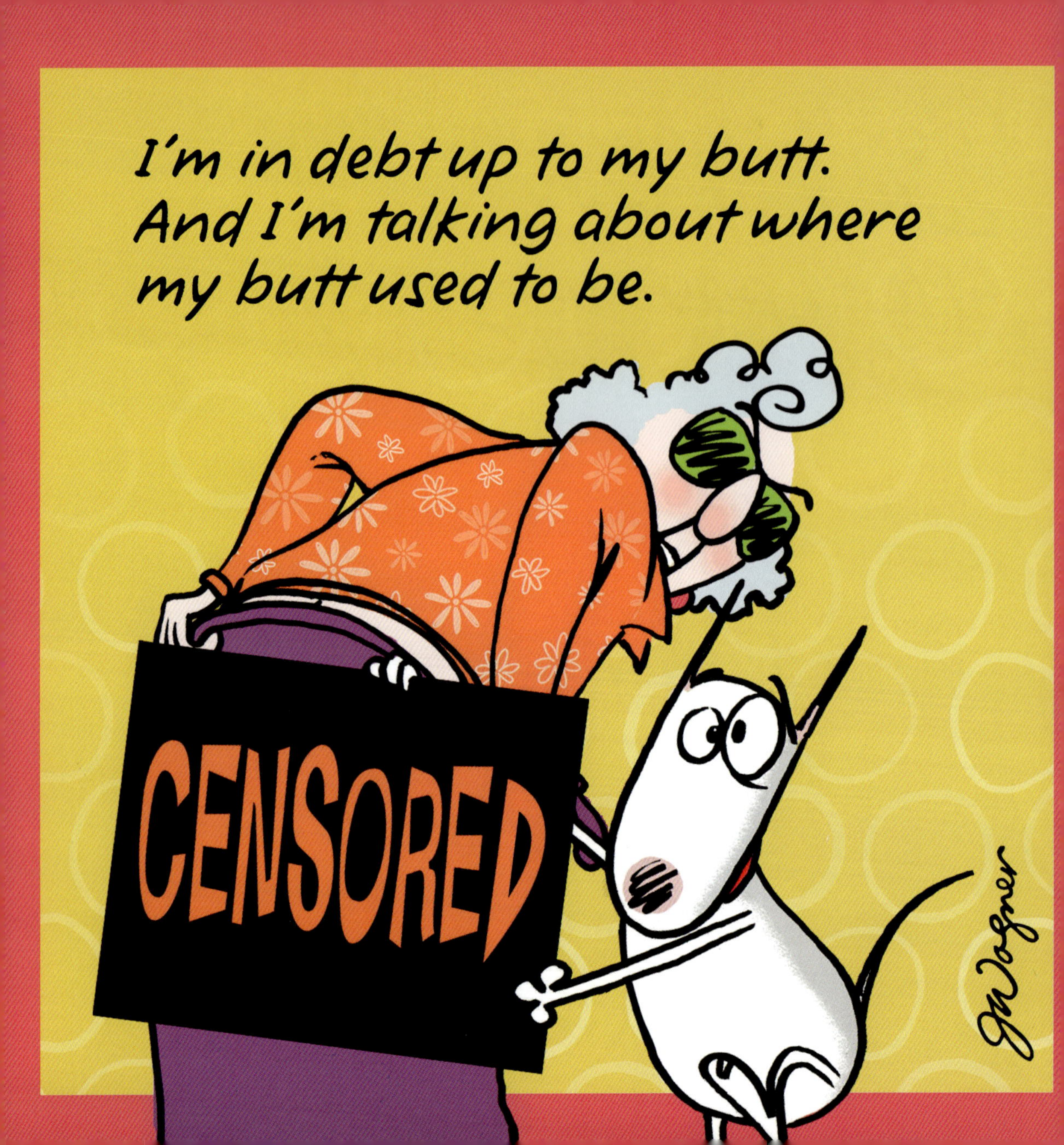
I'm in debt up to my butt.
And I'm talking about where
my butt used to be.
CENSORED

The price of gas is like a pair of cheap underwear. Every time you turn around, it seems to creep up just a little.
CRABBY1

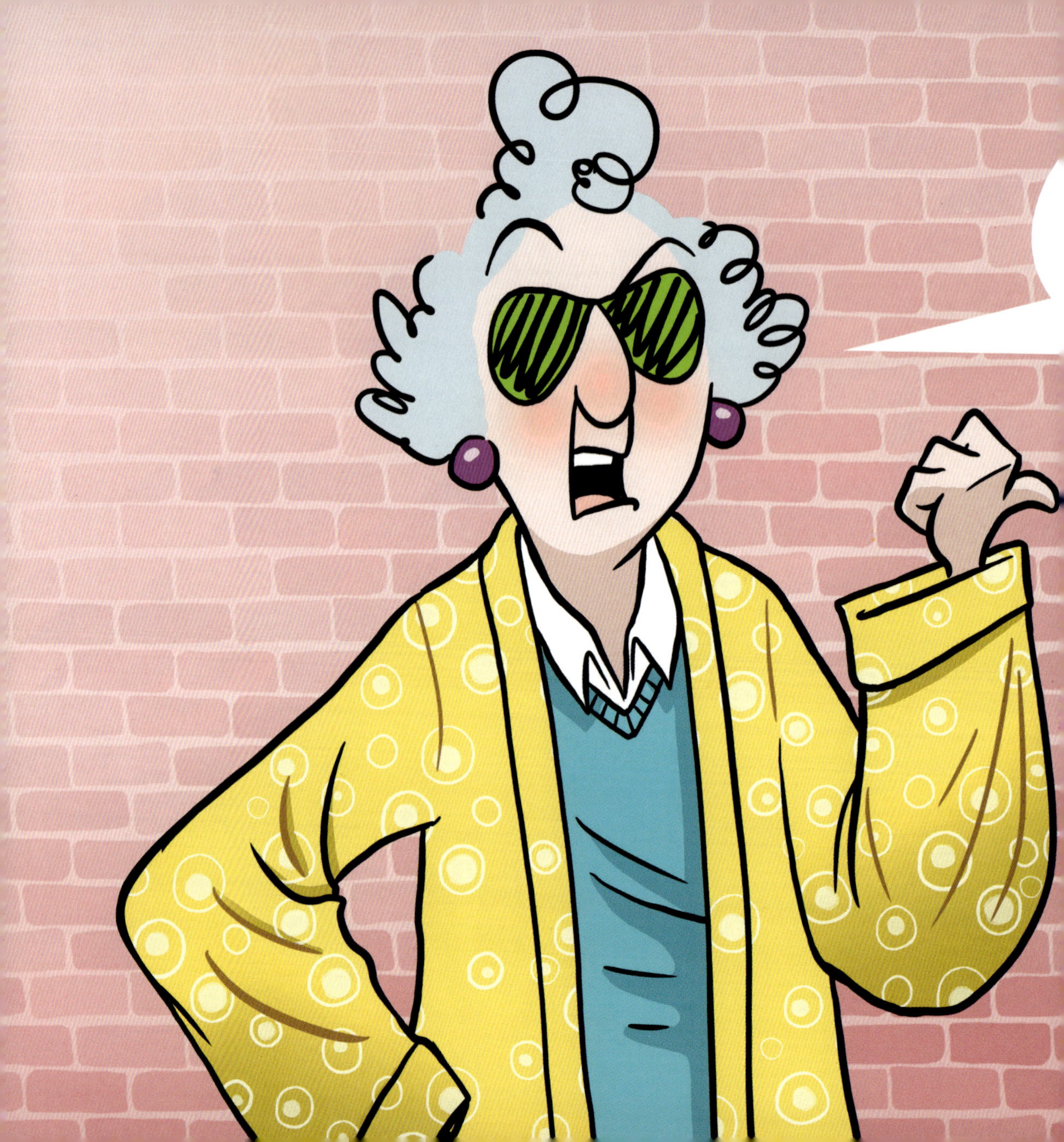

Is it just me, or does this ATM giggle a little every time I make a withdrawal?
ATM
JM Wagner

The bank loans you money one time,
and you pay them every
month for the rest of your life.
Sounds fair.
JWagner

I found a way to save on airline baggage fees. Of course, it's kind of a tight squeeze to sit in one of those cramped seats wearing 12 outfits.
JWagner

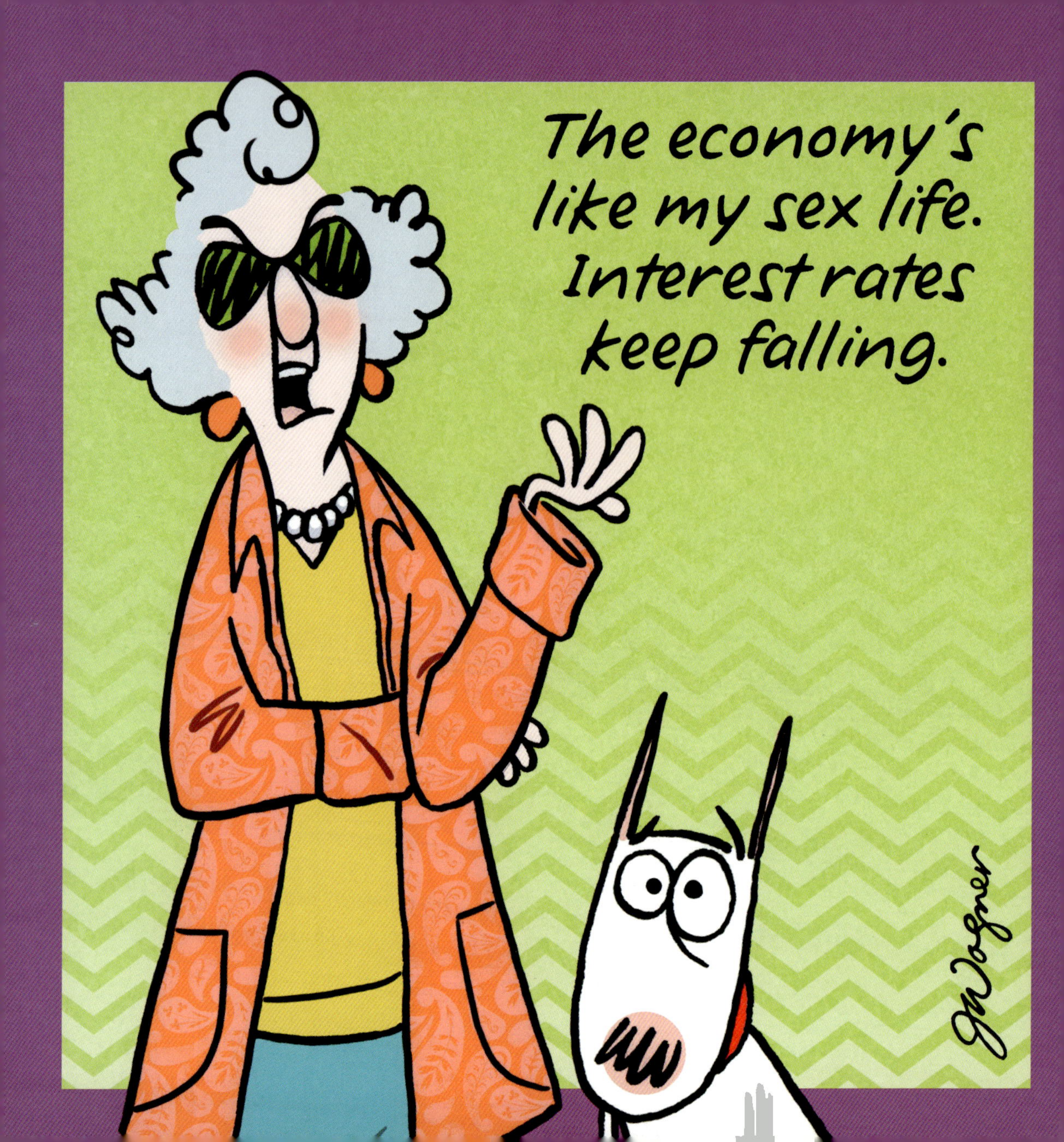
The economy's like my sex life. Interest rates keep falling.

There's nothing wrong
with my paycheck
that a couple
more zeroes
wouldn't cure.
ATM

If I stretched a dollar any further, Washington would look like he's had a facelift.
JWagner

Not only is the economy on its last legs, but I think somebody just kicked it in the shins.
GOVERNMENT REPORT
JWagner

And Now a

Word About Technology...
#@%&!

Being old, old, old school, I'm willing to admit I'm somewhat technologically challenged. I miss the old days when "text" referred to words in a book and the only wall I posted stuff to was in my office. But I guess there's no turning back the clock, especially nowadays, when you have to download the freakin' instructions off the Internet just to learn how to do it.

Tough decision. Do I buy one of those robot vacuums now or hold off until they can do a few more chores?
CHiPS
JWagner

I'm a social media pioneer. I've been unfriending people since back in the '50s.
JWagner

We used to have village idiots, but with the Internet, they've gone global.
I ♥ MY ATTITUDE PROBLEM
JWagner

Gee, I sure feel sorry for all the people tweeting from their smart phones about how hard their lives are.
JWagner

TV is full of sex
and violence.
Fortunately,
I can record two
shows at once!
JWagner

Is there a phone app that stops people from showing you their phone apps?

I won't get up to change the channel, but I'll turn an entire room upside down looking for the remote.
JWagner

I'll retake the driving test as soon as everyone else retakes the turn-off-your-phone-and-pay-attention test.
JWagner

I fed the pigeons in the park once. Does that count as a "Twitter" feed?
JWagner

I thought about getting one of those rechargeable electric cars, but heck, I can't even remember to charge my cell phone.
JWagner

Eventually they're going to have to stop inventing bigger TVs and start inventing bigger walls.
JWagner

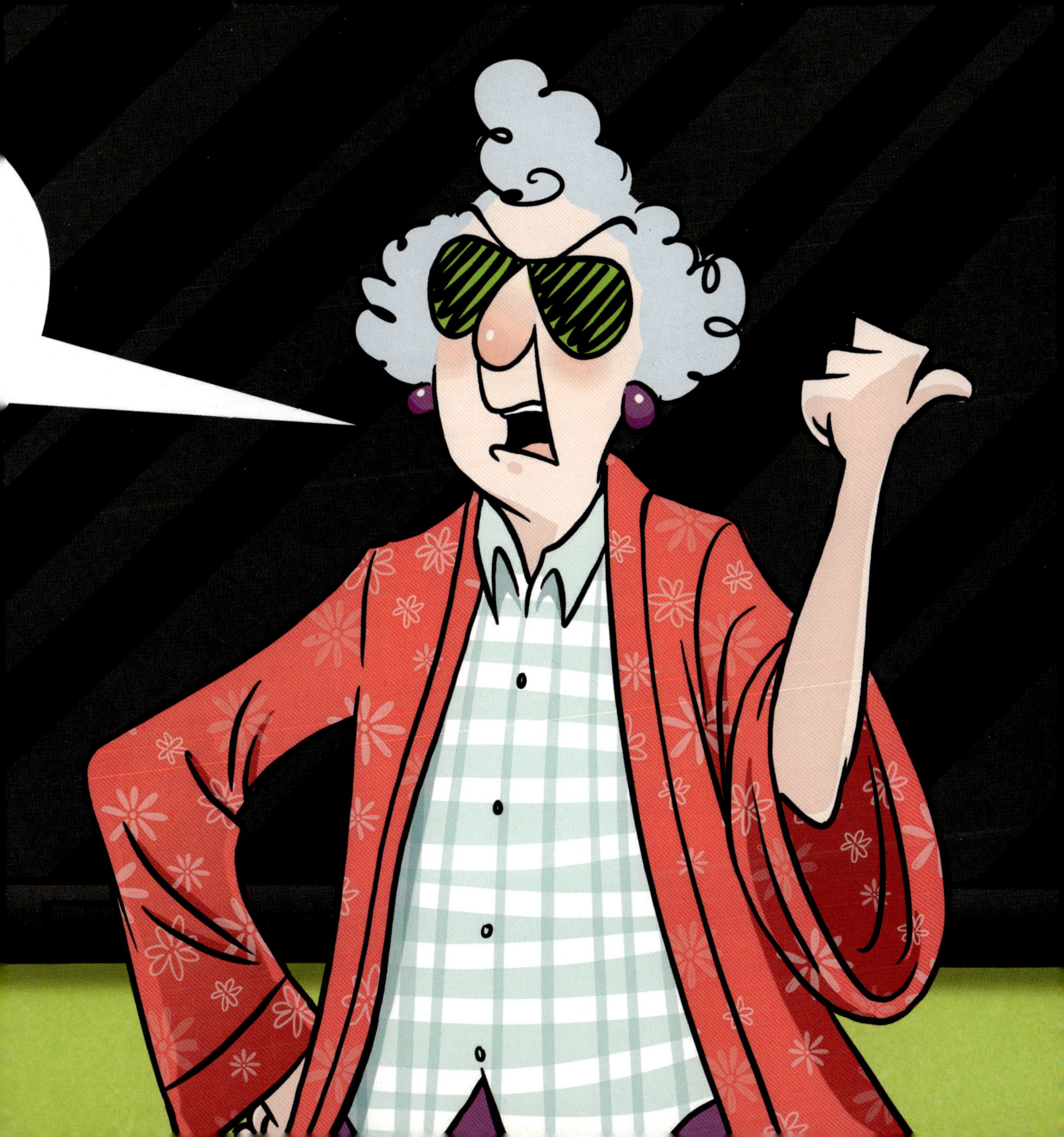

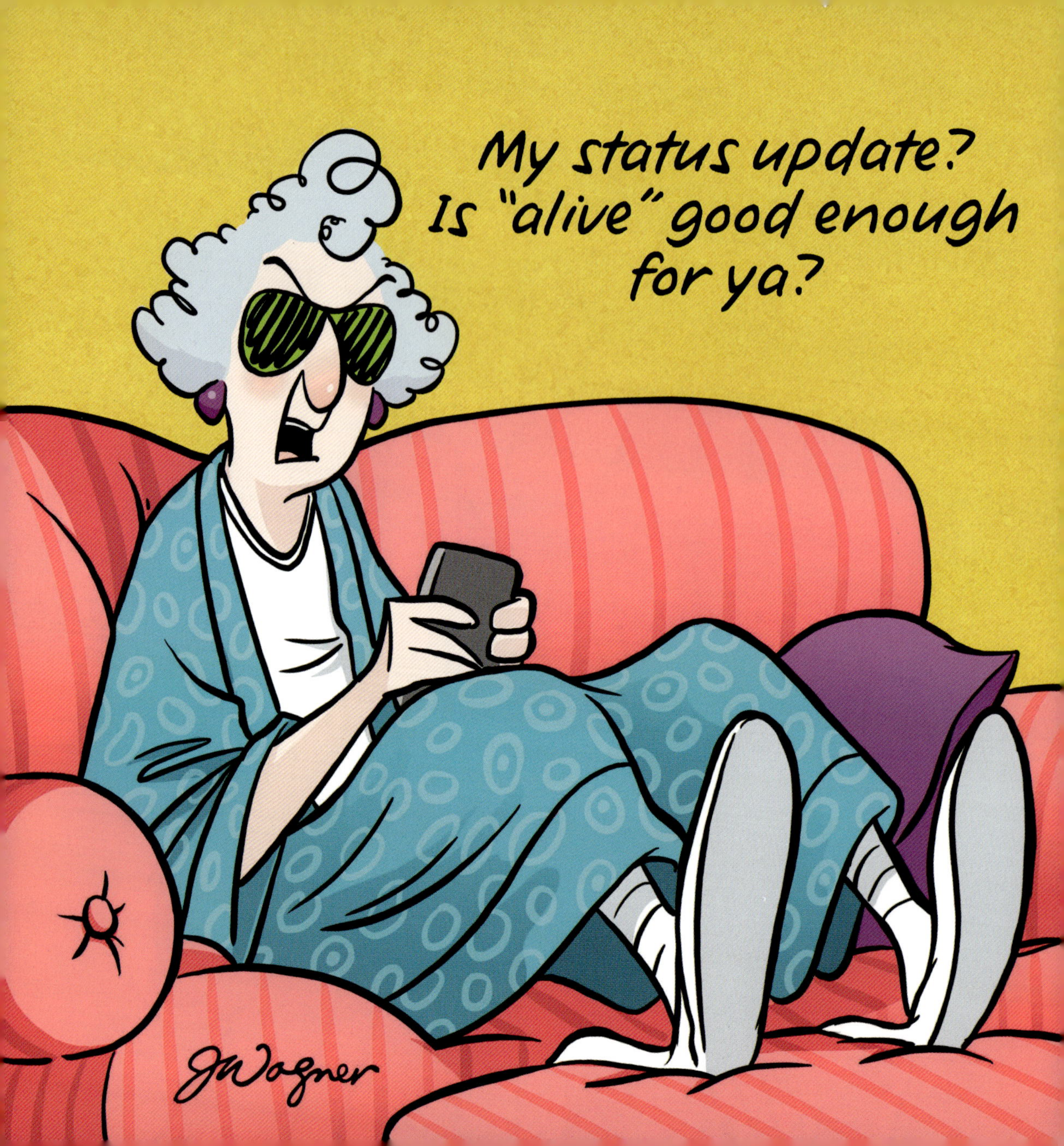
My status update? Is "alive" good enough for ya?
JWagner

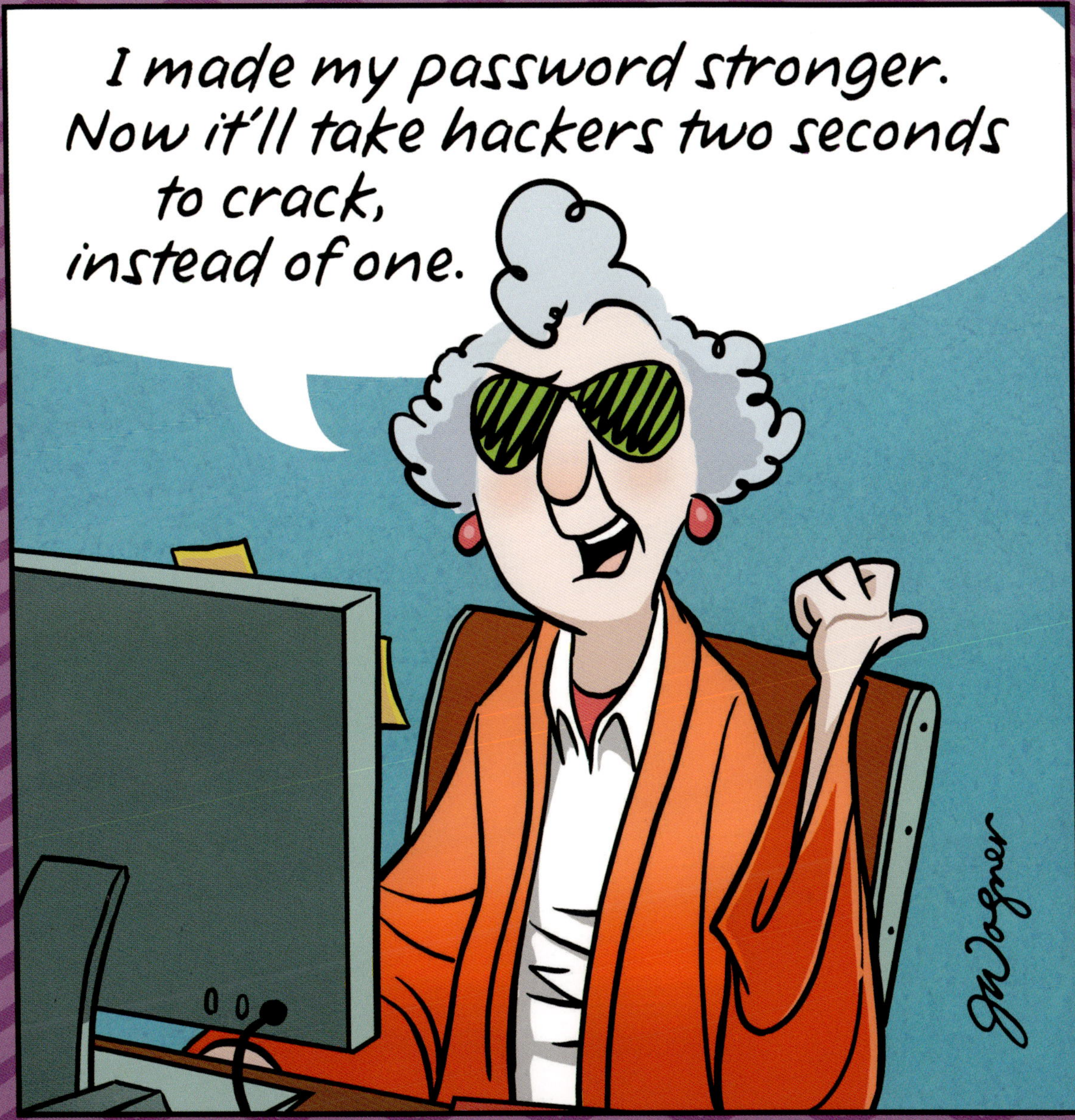
I made my password stronger. Now it'll take hackers two seconds to crack, instead of one.

All it takes to get famous these days is a webcam, boredom, and an ugly cat.

If you liked this book,
or it has touched your life in some way,
we would love to hear from you.

Please send your comments to:
Hallmark Book Feedback
P.O. Box 419034
Mail Drop 100
Kansas City, MO 64141

Or e-mail us at:
booknotes@hallmark.com